SAVAGE:
Totally
Awesome

Other Bantam Starfire Books you will enjoy

FRED SAVAGE:

Totally Awesome

GRACE CATALANO

BANTAM BOOKS
NEW YORK • TORONTO • LONDON • SYDNEY • AUCKLAND

RL 5, age 10 and up

FRED SAVAGE: TOTALLY AWESOME
A Bantam Book / February 1991

*The Starfire logo is a registered trademark of Bantam Books, a division of
Bantam Doubleday Dell Publishing Group, Inc. Registered in U.S. Patent
and Trademark Office and elsewhere.*

ISBN 0-553-28858-X

Published simultaneously in the United States and Canada

*Bantam Books are published by Bantam Books, a division of Bantam
Doubleday Dell Publishing Group, Inc. Its trademark, consisting of the
words "Bantam Books" and the portrayal of a rooster, is Registered in U.S.
Patent and Trademark Office and in other countries. Marca Registrada.
Bantam Books, 666 Fifth Avenue, New York, New York 10103.*

PRINTED IN THE UNITED STATES OF AMERICA

RAD   0 9 8 7 6 5 4 3 2 1

For Ra-Ree

CONTENTS

· 1 ·

BOY WONDER

Fred Savage has taken the entertainment world by storm. Everyone seems to find something to like about him. Between his contagious smile and expressive eyes, remarkable acting talent and charming personality, Fred has emerged as the most lovable young star in Hollywood.

Fred captured the hearts of audiences from the first day he began playing the 1960s kid, Kevin Arnold, on TV's highly rated Emmy-award-winning series, *The*

Wonder Years. But it wasn't the first time Fred acted before the camera. By the time he started working on *The Wonder Years* at age twelve, Fred had already appeared in more than seventy television commercials, numerous television movies, and three motion pictures, *The Boy Who Could Fly, The Princess Bride,* and *Vice Versa*.

Since hitting it big on *The Wonder Years,* Fred has squeezed in two more movies, *Little Monsters* and *The Wizard,* which were both filmed during hiatuses from the show. Fred Savage is in demand. He is adored by teenage girls and admired by adults, who find a little of themselves in Fred's portrayal of Kevin Arnold.

Praises and plaudits for Fred Savage come from all directions. He has been called "the most talented teen on television" by many critics. Carol Black, who with Neal Marlens created *The Wonder Years,* has said that Fred has more concentration than any actor she's worked with.

But who *is* Fred Savage? He seemed to spring up from out of nowhere to be welcomed with open arms. What is his appeal with the viewing public? And why can't anyone get enough of him? Fred is an exciting young star who projects style and a certain kind of magic all his own.

He has been dazzled by the glitz of Hollywood but hasn't let it change him. When he is off the set, he is a regular kid—"just plain Fred" is how he describes himself. He helps out with household chores, plays sports and video games with friends, listens to his favorite music, and collects memorabilia ranging from baseball cards to World War II pins.

Fred says if he ever started acting like a star at home, his family would be the first to let him know and set everything straight. "My mom threatens to take my CD player away or take my baseball cards away," he confesses, then adds with a smile, "That always works."

But Fred's folks don't have to worry too much about Hollywood changing their son. With the help of his family, Fred keeps all his priorities straight. He has been raised in a close-knit, loving family environment and owes his levelheadedness to his mom and dad.

His dad says, "Fred is your typical kid. Whenever he comes home from a project, he fits in pretty well. He has his buddies over, and they run around like regular kids."

His mom says, "Fred is insightful and charismatic and observant." Even his younger sister, Kala, says of her big brother, "Fred is cute and a great actor. I think the expressions on his face are real good—even when he's not talking."

What magic formula does Fred have for success? Though he admits there isn't one, he feels that good timing is just as important as talent. He also feels you have to be prepared for long hours of hard work. And Fred knows what he's talking about. He was only six years old when he entered the highly competitive world of show business.

In just a few years, Fred proved his versatility as an actor and joined the ranks of the entertainment world's "overnight discoveries." His face has become one of the most familiar on television, and he is rapidly becoming a big box-office name on the silver screen as well. Success stories abound in Hollywood, but Fred's seems bona fide. While some actors pound the pavement searching for work, Fred has only gone on a few auditions.

Despite his great accomplishments, Fred always manages to get across the fact that he's keeping his ego in check. "To me, acting is just like a hobby," he says. "It's what I do. I'm just a normal kid doing something I like to do. It definitely doesn't make me better than anyone else!"

His superstardom still astonishes him and his family. With his younger siblings, Kala and Ben, also acting, Fred's mom is trying to keep things at home as normal as possible for her ambitious children.

"It amazes me how all this happened," she says. "We are not an acting family, we just went to auditions. We are just so normal."

Today Fred Savage is a seasoned professional loved by millions of fans. Yet he admits he is a fan himself of so many great actors. When he is invited to award shows or premieres, it is Fred who will go up to another star and express his admiration.

"Last year at the People's Choice Awards, I was too embarrassed to introduce myself to Dustin Hoffman, but I went up to Eddie Murphy," he begins. "I said, 'Hello, Mr. Murphy' and told him he was really funny. And he told me *I* was really funny, too."

While that experience was thrilling for Fred, his favorite moment was meeting actor Clint Eastwood at the Golden Globe Awards. When Fred talks about his encounter with Mr. Eastwood, he imitates the actor's whispery trademark voice and says, "When I met him he said, 'I really like your show, kid. I watch it all the time.'"

Fred continually breaks records by being the youngest performer to accomplish new goals. He was the youngest actor *ever* to be nominated for a best-actor Emmy Award. Even though he didn't win (*Empty Nest*'s Richard Mulligan won), it was truly one of the highlights of Fred's career—so far.

On February 24, 1990, another one of Fred's dreams came true when he guest-hosted *Saturday Night Live*. In this case he was the second-youngest host after Drew Barrymore, who hosted the show in 1982 when she was seven years old. Fred wasn't even born when *Saturday Night Live* started back in 1975, but he says, "I'm a big fan of the show. A lot of times I baby-sit on Saturday night and the parents are out, so I get to watch it. I've been wanting to host it ever since I've seen it." The night Fred hosted, *Saturday Night Live* broke records by drawing the highest ratings since January 1988.

Fred was also one of the hosts of the *People's Choice*

Awards Show and the first cohost on *The Arsenio Hall Show*. He won the job in a Super Bowl bet he made with Arsenio, and the prize was sitting next to the talk-show host for one entire show.

Before Arsenio did the stint with Fred, he jokingly told one reporter, "I've already warned Fred that he'll be in serious trouble if he's better than me. The toughest bully in his school won't be nearly as hard on him as I will."

Of course, it was all in fun. In fact, everything Fred gets involved in turns out to be fun. When he speaks about the business he's chosen to be part of, Fred asserts, "I don't do this to be competitive. I don't do it to be popular or have fans. I do it for fun. I'm acting because I enjoy it, and if I ever stopped having fun, I'd stop acting."

That doesn't seem likely in the years ahead. *The Wonder Years* has made Fred Savage a major star. It's established him with fellow actors who respect him and admire his talent, and the experience has opened doors for even more movie roles. Fred Savage has achieved what all actors dream of. He's become a star with a brilliant future ahead of him.

·2·

THE COMMERCIAL KID

Fred Aaron Savage was born on a hot, sunny day in Highland Park, Illinois, a suburb of Chicago. The date was July 9, 1976, although he was scheduled to be born on July 4. Fred was the first child born to Lew and Joanne Savage. In the next four years, Fred's sister, Kala, and brother, Ben, joined the family.

Fred grew up in a house filled with love and caring and kindness. He was a happy and good baby who was always smiling and who rarely cried.

Fred spent the first five years of his life the way most kids do. He loved being outdoors in the sun, playing sports and games with his friends. Adorable Fred was the perfect example of an all-American kid.

He remembers that his first ambition was "to be a professional baseball player." No one envisioned that the young, bright-eyed boy would enter show business in such a short time. Though it seems common for kids to dream of starring in a hit movie or smash television series someday, the thought hadn't occurred to Fred Savage. Acting didn't run in his family. His mom claims, "I was never even in a school play."

But one day all that was to change for Fred and his family. He was five years old and attending kindergarten classes half a day. He remembers one morning all the kids were buzzing about local auditions being held in the community center for an Oscar Meyer hot dog commercial.

Fred listened to the kids who were going to try out after school. The thrill of possibly winning the commercial role was too exciting for anyone to ignore. And Fred wasn't about to be the only kid in school not to audition.

That afternoon he asked his mom to drive him to the community center. She agreed, but only because all the other mothers in town were doing it. "It wasn't like we were starting a career for Fred," says Joanne. "It was just a lot of mothers, instead of going to the park that day after school, I took the kids to the center.

If it had been in Chicago, I wouldn't have gone. But it was close to our home, so I figured I'd take him."

Fred knew nothing about acting. In fact, when he tried out for the hot dog commercial, he said, "All I knew how to do was eat them." He remembers that first audition as being "fun": "Even though I didn't get the role, I still thought it was a lot of fun."

That first audition began Fred's career. He left an indelible impression on the director of the commercial who couldn't get the perky, energetic youngster out of his mind. In one year Fred Savage would enter the world of acting, though he didn't know it at the time. All he knew was that he liked the excitement of auditioning and wanted to continue trying out for future parts.

Although Fred had the support and encouragement of his family, his mother wasn't totally convinced that Fred should get into acting. She knew the competition would be rough, and that dozens of aspirants fail for every one who succeeds. A casting director may audition scores of young applicants before deciding on the one who will get the job.

Fred was only five years old, and his mother felt he was too young to experience rejection. However, he was ready to audition again, and six months after the auditions for the hot-dog commercial, the same director called Fred in for a Pizza Hut commercial he was casting.

Although he did his best, Fred still lost the role. He

would have to wait another six months to get his lucky break at last. Again, the same director asked to see Fred. This time he was casting a Pac-Man vitamin commercial. Being a video-game fanatic, Fred was most excited about this audition, and his performance was inspired enough to win the role.

Now Fred claims, "I did my first commercial because I liked video games. If the ad was for something else, like Hanes underwear, I probably wouldn't have wanted to do it, and I wouldn't be here today."

When asked how he felt when he won the vitamin spot, Fred says, "I was very excited. No kid I knew was ever on TV before." The commercial introduced Pac-Man vitamins to kids, and Fred remembers his first line as an actor to this day. With a big smile and a twinkle in his saucer-shaped brown eyes, he recites, "Good-bye Fred [a reference to Fred Flintstones vitamins], hello Pac-Man!"

One look at Fred on-screen was all it took to convince producers and directors he was on his way to bigger things. The phones started ringing off the hook for Fred to appear in more commercials. Over the next two and a half years, he filmed over seventy television ads for everything from toys to detergent to breakfast cereal.

Though shooting commercials was a great training ground for the budding young actor, Fred found the experience repetitious. Whenever he was scheduled to film a commercial, he would have to do the same thing over and over even though each ad was for something different. If it was for cereal, he'd have to eat many spoonfuls of it until the director was satisfied.

Fred grew tired of doing commercials and wanted to move on, but he was still so young. There were very few parts in both television and movies for someone his age. So he continued to film commercials, and he also won a few stints doing voice-overs, or recording his voice for a commercial even though he wasn't seen on camera.

When Fred Savage was seven years old, his parents felt they couldn't deny his seriousness about acting. Fred was already a two-year veteran of the business, and he planned on going even further. Many times his parents told him he didn't have to act after school. His mom says, "I've told him, 'You don't have to do this; we'll love you even if you don't do this.' But Fred wants to act, he loves it."

His dad adds, "Ever since Fred was six, he always wanted to go on auditions. You could pull him off a baseball field, or camp, or a party—he never blinked."

Though he had become a favorite "commercial kid," both his parents knew it was time for Fred to try his hand at acting in movies and television. The only problem for the Savages was their location. They lived in Glencoe, right outside the city of Chicago, far from New York and California, where most auditions are held. They assured Fred's agent it wouldn't be a problem. They were ready to travel for auditions—if the right part came along.

The idea of playing different characters excited young Fred Savage, and roles in movies and television were not far from his reach. Even without formal training, Fred showed a natural ability and flair for his craft. His next audition would be vital for his budding career.

·3·

THE BOY WHO COULD ACT

Fred Savage made his motion-picture debut as Louis Michaelson in the 1986 film, *The Boy Who Could Fly*. For the excited eight-year-old, winning a role in this movie was a dream come true. It gave him the opportunity to channel all his energy and acting abilities into one project. Fred wasn't the star of the movie, but his role was pivotal to the story.

The Boy Who Could Fly was the complete invention of writer/director Nick Castle. The initial idea for the story came to Castle when he was reading *Dumbo* to his seven-year-old son, Louis. He decided to write an outline about a strange, awkward boy, a character who would send a message to viewers about believing in their dreams. "We need to believe in magic to get by all the big and small tragedies that happen in life," says Castle, who also directed *The Last Starfighter*. "That's what I wanted *The Boy Who Could Fly* to be about."

It is the story of the Michaelsons, a family facing a financial dilemma after the loss of their father. Having given up their home and moved to a new neighborhood, the mother encounters difficulty in her attempt to return to work after a ten-year absence.

Her fourteen-year-old daughter, Milly, has her own adjustments—trying to fit in at a new school and taking on the household responsibilities. Louis, her eight-year-old brother, whose only friend is his dog Max, is trying to deal with the loss of his father and the constant threat from the bullies who live on his block.

Their new neighbor is Eric Gibb, a boy Milly's age, who sits perched on the windowsill of his room, arms outstretched pretending to fly. He was orphaned at age five and raised by a caring, yet eccentric, uncle. The main story of *The Boy Who Could Fly* is the relationship between Eric and Milly. The movie's theme—that you can soar above everyday problems—sparks the viewers' imaginations.

When Nick Castle began casting the film, he saved

the role of the little brother, Louis, for close to last. He wasn't sure he was going to find a child actor who could play the part the way he envisioned it.

So first he went ahead and cast the roles of Eric and Milly. Jay Underwood, who at the time was attending the Children's Theatre School in Minneapolis, didn't have much professional acting experience, having played only a small role in the Jon Voight movie, *Desert Bloom*. But Castle says, "An agent sent us a tape of Jay, and we immediately knew he was Eric. The sensitivity and innocence were there."

In the role of Milly, Castle cast Lucy Deakins, at the time a regular on the soap opera *As the World Turns*. "Her role is crucial to the film, as she is in just about every scene," says Castle. "In her tests we gave her the toughest ones to do. Not only did she have the ability to act them, but she put forth a variety of emotions."

Next came the role of Louis Michaelson. Castle will never forget the first time he saw precocious little Fred Savage. Beaming with a kidlike delight, Castle says, "For the little brother, Louis, we stumbled onto a real crazy and wonderful little guy named Fred Savage. Again, I was viewing one of a hundred tapes sent to us. Suddenly this head popped up on the screen with this weird hair sticking straight up and this picket-fence smile. My immediate reaction was, 'Get this kid out here.'"

In a matter of a few days, Fred and his parents were on a plane to California. Before deciding on Fred as his final choice for the role, Nick Castle wanted to meet him and screen-test him.

Fred remembers the experience as being a little nerve-racking. "It was my first audition for a movie, and I was a little nervous," he says, "but like the guy says in the TV commercial—'Never let them see you sweat.'"

Nick Castle later said of Fred, "He was just as wonderful as I thought he would be. Just as adorable in person, if not more so." After screen-testing Fred, there was no doubt in Castle's mind that he possessed just the right qualities to portray the role of Louis. With a quick stroke of his pen, he cast Fred in his first film role.

Rounding out the cast of *The Boy Who Could Fly* were Bonnie Bedelia as Charlene, the mother of Milly and Louis; Fred Gwynne as Eric's Uncle Hugo; Colleen Dewhurst as Mrs. Sherman, Eric and Milly's teacher; Louise Fletcher as Dr. Granada, a psychiatrist who counsels Milly on her vivid imagination, and Mindy Cohn from the TV series *The Facts of Life* as Milly's best friend, Geneva.

The reality of Fred winning a role in a movie was very exciting to the Savage family, and they were ready to make any adjustments necessary. The movie, which was filmed in Vancouver, British Columbia, Canada, required that Fred temporarily move to that location, but Fred's mother, younger brother, and younger sister moved too and were with him the entire time he was in Vancouver. Although Fred's mom was able to get a leave of absence from her job as an industrial real-estate broker, it wasn't that easy for Fred's dad.

Lew Savage, who also works in industrial real estate, couldn't get much time off from his job, so he stayed in Chicago. He did fly to Vancouver on weekends to spend time with his family.

At the time of production, Fred's mother said, "We want Fred to have a normal childhood. This was something he wanted to do, and we want him to do it. So, for all of us, we're making it a family project."

Throughout the filming of *The Boy Who Could Fly*, Nick Castle kept a keen eye on Fred. The young boy had never taken an acting lesson and had only previously appeared in television commercials. Yet he was extremely talented and had the ability to play both drama and comedy.

"In the picture Fred has to play a kid his own age who deals with the mystifying loss of his father by attempting to emulate the solitary code of his GI Joe toy soldiers," says Nick Castle. "It was amazing how much of a professional he was. He could handle a comic scene as well as a heavy dramatic one with ease; and he still had plenty of energy left to clown around the set with the crew."

In interviews Fred was very vocal, speaking about many things including his director, Nick Castle. "He is really a nice guy," said Fred. "We play things like thumb wars and Indian wrestling. We have a pretty great time together on the set."

Fred described his character, Louis, as "all sorts of stuff. He's like sad and happy, and he's just like from another world. I think he's a neat kid."

When asked to describe himself, he said with a grin, "I think Fred Savage is smart, a fun guy, hopeful. I guess pretty happy, and I think the way I should put it, wild and crazy, but nice, too."

Fred's performance in *The Boy Who Could Fly* was very well received. He won his first Youth-in-Film Award for best supporting actor for his sensitive portrayal of Louis. Producers and casting directors who didn't know him started asking about him. Over the next year Fred would have very little time off as he began winning several roles that gave him exposure, recognition, and valuable experience.

In the short-lived TV series, *Morningstar/Eveningstar,* Fred made his television debut playing Alan, one of a group of orphans who lose their orphanage and move in with elderly people living in a retirement home. In one very touching episode, Alan and his sister, Sarah, also an orphan (played by Missy Francis) are to be adopted by Judge and Jenna Lindsay (Joshua Bruant and Donna Mitchell) after the couple become obsessed with Alan's resemblance to their deceased son. The hour-long drama, which touched on serious issues, wasn't the hit CBS had hoped it would be, and it was canceled after only one season on the air.

Fred was disappointed over the cancellation of *Morningstar/Eveningstar,* so it was fortunate that other offers were coming his way. Fred next appeared in a string of television projects, including a guest-starring role on an episode of *The Twilight Zone* and starring roles in the TV movies *Convicted: A Mother's Story* with Ann Jillian, *Run 'Til You Fall* with Jamie Farr, and an ABC-TV weekend special *Runaway Ralph,* in which Fred befriends a talking mouse.

This nonstop work brought Fred and his family to Los Angeles temporarily. In between gigs he flew back to his home in Glencoe to see his friends and go back to regular school.

When he returned home for the first time after appearing on the big and small screens, Fred found little difference in the way his friends treated him. He was glad because he didn't want his acting career to interfere with his hometown life. Sure, his friends asked him questions about the movie and television world and living in California, but once he told them what they wanted to know, it was back to normal.

Fred had always been popular in school, and when he made a friend, he always hoped it would be for life. To this day he says with a proud smile, "I've had the same friends since I was two years old." He was happy to see when he returned home that no one was waiting to roll out the red carpet for the "new star."

Although Fred has always come across as happy and positive, he did go through the usual growing pains like everyone else. He just learned at a very young age how to adjust to changes, so that he could handle whatever was handed to him with ease.

The first thing Fred did when he returned home was join the Little League team because of his love for baseball. Although later Fred would describe himself as "a horrible baseball player," he did have a few good days on the baseball field. He'll always remember the first time he hit the ball far enough to advance to first base.

When he recalls that first special moment, he says, "I remember I closed my eyes, stuck the bat out, and felt something vibrate. So I ran like crazy!"

Fred's return home brought him back to life as a regular kid—going to school, having friends over to the house, and playing sports on weekends. After filming the movie, it was a very different world for Fred, one that was much more carefree.

But back in Hollywood things were happening that Fred wasn't even aware of, and his stay in Glencoe was to be a short one. Once all the TV work he had done was aired, producers wondered why the sensational work of this young actor had been kept under wraps. Suddenly Fred's name began to crop up as the choice for roles in movies and television. At just ten years old, Fred Savage was already a confident and accomplished actor, and everyone was interested in him.

All this attention marked the beginning for him. Stardom was a way off yet, but people were taking notice of Fred Savage, and that meant only one thing: He was on his way to the top!

·4·

THE PRINCESS BRIDE

There are very few wholesome, well-scrubbed, all-American child actors who reach the success Fred Savage has achieved. He has charmed audiences with every one of his performances and touched the world like no other young actor has.

Fred delivers his lines with great timing. He completely dedicates himself to his roles, and both audiences and critics love him. These qualities impressed director Rob Reiner so much that he cast Fred as the grandson in his magical sleeper hit movie, *The Princess Bride*.

This unique film blended together the talents of an impressive ensemble cast including Carl Elwes, Mandy Patinkin, Peter Falk, Carol Kane, Billy Crystal, Christopher Guest, and Chris Sarandon. *The Princess Bride,* a spirited, comic tale of true love and high adventure, was based on the best-selling novel by William Goldman. The executive producer was Norman Lear, and the director was Rob Reiner.

Fred couldn't believe he was going to work with Reiner, whose credits include the hit movies *Stand by Me, This Is Spinal Tap, The Sure Thing,* and *When Harry Met Sally.* . . . Yet while that was exciting enough, Fred was equally pleased to find out that his scenes were to be played opposite veteran actor Peter Falk, best known for his portrayal of the famous television lieutenant Columbo.

In the movie Fred plays a young boy bedridden with the flu, who is less than thrilled when his grandfather arrives to read aloud the book *The Princess Bride*. Though he appears to be hard to impress, Fred's character, just called "grandson," becomes engrossed in the characters of the book.

As the story comes to life, the movie's action is transported from the boy's modern bedroom to a mystical land from centuries ago. As his grandfather begins to read the adventures of Buttercup, the most beautiful woman in the world, and Westley, the man she loves, the fairy-tale kingdom of Florin fills the screen. And the adventure begins. Actually, the movie is two separate stories: the love story between Westley and Buttercup, and the story of Inigo Montaya, who is out to avenge the death of his father.

Though Fred appears in only a few scenes of *The Princess Bride,* the film is really told through his consciousness, depicting how he imagines what his grandfather is reading.

Rob Reiner says, "The most important thing for me in the script is the little boy, who is reluctant to see his grandfather and is brought closer to him by the end of the film as a result of having had this story read to him."

The idea for *The Princess Bride* began when William Goldman set out to tell his two young daughters a fairy tale before bedtime. He explains: "I said to my daughters, 'I'll write you a story. What do you want it to be about?' And one said, 'Princesses,' and the other said, 'Brides.' I said, 'Okay, *The Princess Bride* will be the title.' It started out to be a children's book, but then I ran dry of ideas for a children's book and got the notion of going from good part to good part, omitting the boring parts."

The movie holds a very special place in everyone's heart from Rob Reiner to William Goldman to Fred and the rest of the cast to the film's producer, Andrew Scheinman. "I don't know of any other film like this," says Scheinman. "The only film that's remotely similar in tone is *Butch Cassidy and the Sundance Kid* [also written by William Goldman], where they looked like cowboys and rode like cowboys, but they didn't always talk like cowboys. In *The Princess Bride* they look like the people we've seen in swashbuckling epics. They dress and move and do everything else like that, but they don't always talk like that. I think that's what makes it so special."

Fred enjoyed playing his role in *The Princess Bride*. He especially liked the fact that the movie was shot in England because it gave him and his family the chance to see London for the first time. Filmed primarily at Lee International Studios in Shepperton, England, the additional locations took place in Derbyshire and Kent.

"It was great," says Fred. "Filming that movie in England was a lot of fun and one of the best experiences I've had as an actor."

With only a few TV roles and one other feature film under his belt, Fred seemed right at home in front of the camera. He found acting to be easy from the beginning. "I don't know how I learned to act," he says. "I think that everyone acts. When you're sarcastic, you're acting. When you're acting funny for people, you're acting. I'm just doing it in movies and television."

The first two films Fred appeared in were critical and commercial successes. He won his second Youth-in-Film Award for his role in *The Princess Bride,* this time nabbing best young actor in a motion picture. His track record was unbelievable. He wondered if it would continue.

Fred seemed to be the one part of his films that critics liked best. Word began to spread around Hollywood that Fred's talent was being wasted as long as producers weren't starring him in his own movie.

Everything was moving so fast, Fred didn't even think about winning a leading role. Then again, he didn't *have* to think about it because he would soon be playing the lead character in his next film, *Vice Versa*.

·5·

STARRING
FRED SAVAGE

By the time Fred Savage appeared on the silver screen in *Vice Versa*, his face had become very familiar to audiences. The movie meant a lot to Fred for several reasons, the most important being that it was filmed in Chicago. For the first time since Fred began acting, he was able to stay in his own house while working on a movie. He was getting tired of hotels and restaurants and just wanted to sleep in his own bed and eat a home-cooked meal.

The movie was not only Fred's first comedy, but also his first major role in a film. His character would appear throughout the film instead of just filling in gaps as he had done in *The Boy Who Could Fly* and *The Princess Bride*. This movie would rest primarily on the shoulders of Fred and Judge Reinhold, whom he shared star credit with.

The relationship between these two actors is very important to the story. The characters are a contemporary father and son, and the story is straightforward and humanistic, but with an interesting twist.

In *Vice Versa* Fred plays Charlie Seymour, the eleven-year-old son of Marshall Seymour (played by Judge Reinhold), executive vice president in one of Chicago's most prestigious department stores. Marshall is a divorced, stressed-out workaholic with little time for his son.

The two suddenly find themselves under the influence of a mystical skull. They seem to have become closer, but in reality their minds have switched bodies. Fred plays the adult trapped inside a boy's body, while Judge plays a young boy trapped inside a man's body.

One reason why this body-switch comedy works so well is because of the freedom Fred was allowed with his character. The director, Brian Gilbert, knew the movie was based mainly on the relationship between the father and son, and he encouraged creative contributions from the actors. Fred knew he could play his role the way he wanted to. The special touches he added to the character as it was written made him interesting and compelling on-screen.

The premise of the story was funny and charming, and it allowed Fred to prove that he could really do anything. There is no denying the fact that this film was one of Fred's biggest challenges as an actor so far. It is the first movie for which he did some research before plunging into his role. Fred wanted the public to believe that he really was an adult trapped inside the body of a boy, so he started to study adults. He studied his parents and the people who were working on the movie. He watched how they acted, how they carried themselves, and tried to remember all of the details for his scenes.

Fred knew that once the director yelled, "Action," he had to be ready. He had to be prepared to play his part as realistically as he knew how. In preparation for the scenes where Fred switches places with Judge Reinhold's character, he sat down and talked to Reinhold. "Judge and I studied each other as to the different things we did," says Fred. "Sometimes Judge and I would ask each other what we would do if we were in a certain situation, and we would learn that way from each other.

"A lot of times, to get the right emphasis on lines, I'd ask Judge if he could please say the line. Then I'd copy his ups and downs and tone of voice."

Fred did a magnificent job in *Vice Versa*. When the movie was released, it grossed $4 million in its opening weekend. The critics were unanimous in their praise of the film. Roger Ebert of the *Chicago Sun-Times* called it "one of the year's most endearing comedies. A treasure of a movie." Gene Siskel of the *Chicago Tribune* wrote, "funny family entertainment."

Among the people impressed with Fred's performance in *Vice Versa* were two producers named Neal Marlens and Carol Black. They had created the popular TV series, *Growing Pains,* and were now working on another series called *The Wonder Years.* They watched Fred in his third movie and knew right away that he *had* to play the show's lead character, Kevin Arnold.

In less than one year, Fred Savage would become a household name, the hottest preteenage actor on the tube in the hottest new show of the year.

◄ 6 ►

THE WONDER YEARS

Neal Marlens and Carol Black were enthusiastic about *The Wonder Years*. They knew it would work if it was given the right chance. ABC-TV bought the show's pilot as a midseason experiment. The future of the show relied on the pilot. It had to be something the public was not expecting, something fresh, something so different audiences wouldn't be able to wait for the next episode.

Could there be such a show? Marlens, Black, and

ABC-TV sure hoped so. Cocreators, writers, and producers Marlens and Black were a successful team. In 1985 they created *Growing Pains*, a family sitcom starring Alan Thicke and Joanna Kerns as the parents of three kids, played by the then-unknown Kirk Cameron, Tracey Gold, and Jeremy Miller. The show would go on to become the season's biggest success, with Kirk Cameron becoming the country's hottest teen heartthrob.

With *Growing Pains* continually climbing the Nielsen ratings chart, Marlens and Black went back to the drawing board and began working on a new idea for a series. This show would take viewers back to the late 1960s, a time of innocence, but also a time of hippies, flower power, psychedelic music, and the Vietnam War. The show would be set in the suburbs and would be narrated by Kevin Arnold, who, as an adult, looks back on the years when he was growing up. In a half-hour comedy series format, the program would explore the experience of growing up during the late 1960s and early 1970s and would include all the love, tears, and laughter of a family in the memory of the youngest child.

When casting began for *The Wonder Years*, Fred Savage's agent was the first to be called. Marlens and Black explained they had seen Fred's performance in *Vice Versa* and wanted him to read for the part of Kevin Arnold. Fred's agent immediately saw the prospects in the series and sent Fred and his family a script. He was eager for Fred to be part of *The Wonder Years*. The part of Kevin Arnold could easily make someone a star. It was the kind of role that would affect audiences tremendously and would show what the actor could do.

At first Fred didn't want to tie himself to another television series. He liked doing movies and thought he would miss being offered roles on the big screen. He didn't realize then that this part would open even more doors for him. After Fred's parents read the script of *The Wonder Years,* they were anxious for him to audition. They felt it was unique, like nothing else they had read or seen before on television. After reading the script himself, Fred felt the same way.

"First my agent said, 'You have to read *The Wonder Years,*'" remembers Fred. "Then my parents read it and loved it, too. I don't think there are many series that are this good." After Fred flew to California and read for the producers, director, and the people at ABC-TV, he officially won the role.

Since the pilot was scheduled to air on January 31, 1988, filming was to begin immediately after all the roles were cast. The actors chosen to play the rest of the Arnold family were Dan Lauria as Jack, Kevin's dad; Alley Mills as Norma, Kevin's mom; Jason Hervey as his obnoxious older brother, Wayne, and Olivia d'Abo as his sister Karen, who was just entering the love-beads stage of her life, and who exposes her younger brother to the political turmoil of the outer world. Josh Saviano won the part of Paul Pfeiffer,

Kevin's best friend, and Danica McKellar was cast as Winnie Cooper, Kevin's first girlfriend. Together these actors formed a perfect ensemble.

Fred and his mom flew to Southern California, where the pilot for *The Wonder Years* was filmed. He was completely prepared to portray his role—except for one thing! He was nervous about the kissing scene with Danica McKellar in the pilot episode. Fred just wasn't sure what kind of kiss it was supposed to be!

Though it was traumatic for them to do the kissing scene in front of the crew, Fred and Danica had no trouble once the cameras started rolling.

Carol Black remembers, "When we were ready to shoot it, Fred and Danica giggled quite a bit for a couple of minutes and had a hard time stopping. But when we really got down to shoot it, bingo, there it was. They had no problem with it!"

Still, Fred insists, "It was kind of embarrassing. But there was no escaping . . . the show must go on. We skipped over the kiss in rehearsal, but then the time came when we had to do it. The director said, 'Okay, let's do the kiss now.' And I was like, 'Okay, in a minute!' I almost didn't do it. The most embarrassing thing about it was that at the end of the scene my mom and Danica's mom stood up and clapped," Fred adds with a smile.

On January 31, 1988, the first show of *The Wonder Years* debuted on millions of TV screens across the country. At that time no one had any idea what a sensation the young actor who played Kevin Arnold would cause. No one expected *The Wonder Years* to become one of the best shows of the year. But that's exactly what happened.

The Wonder Years was an instant hit—people loved it! The response was overwhelming, and the network ordered more shows. What was extra-special about this show was that it appealed to both kids and adults, who were reminded of their own childhood through Kevin's memory.

Fred commanded a lot of attention in his role. Many critics singled him out, applauding his spunkiness, naturalness, and his flair for handling the part. His appeal is that you believe in him. He puts a lot of himself into his role and appears as a gentle kid with a heart of gold. Overnight Fred Savage became the youngest idol on television.

Fan mail started to pour in by the thousands. Most letters were from nine- to eighteen-year-old girls. They called Fred "cute," "cuddly," and "sexy." Some asked for an autographed photo. Others even proposed a date or marriage. They congratulated him on the show and told him that they never missed an episode.

Fred responded to his fan mail with astonishment. "I think it's great," he said. "It's neat that people you've never met write to you and support your career."

The fan mail was just the beginning of Fred's rise to stardom. He was soon featured in teen magazines, and editors were requesting interviews with him. While his picture graced the covers of scores of magazines, promoters discovered Fred's adorable face could be turned into a salable commodity. Two different color posters of Fred were marketed and sold. Soon Fred's smiling face was appearing everywhere.

How does Fred feel about the heavy media attention? "I definitely feel like a regular kid," he says. "Nothing has changed for me with my family and friends. It's people who don't know me personally who think of me as a star. I'm just a normal kid doing something he likes to do."

Once Fred began appearing in more episodes of *The Wonder Years*, he became interested in learning about the 1960s. The producers thought it would be hard for a child of today to understand what it was like growing up in 1968. Neal Marlens describes it as a time when kids had to choose between idolizing John Wayne or John Lennon. According to Fred, "The Beatles are oldies."

He expresses his feelings about the 1960s by saying, "It was like everybody was struggling. If they had an older son or daughter, they were worried that they'd become hippies, and they were worried about politics and the war. It was a troublesome era, I guess, but it was also a real fun time. I know a little bit about the era from my parents and what I learn in school."

Fred says his favorite president in history is John F. Kennedy. He has read every book about him. Fred also loves the music of the 1950s and 1960s and says he'd like to go back to those years just for one day "to see all the hippies and protesters."

Fred is quick to point out, "The character I play actually doesn't know about the time. Vietnam is going on, but Kevin is more concerned about calling his girlfriend." There are many similarities and differences between Fred and his television alter ego.

"Kevin is a lot like me," he says. "He goes through the same thing. He worries about girls and school and the way his hair looks. The differences between us would be his shyness. I'm a little shy with girls but not as shy as Kevin. And whenever something is going well for him, his older brother, Wayne, tries to ruin it—and I don't have an older brother. Kids of today and kids of the 1960s do different things for fun. I like to play video games, and Kevin plays games outside in the street."

Sometimes an episode comes along that Fred thinks is going to be fun to do, but it turns out to be just the opposite. For example, in one show Kevin and Paul were supposed to try smoking cigarettes. To prepare for the scene, *The Wonder Years* producer gave Fred and costar Josh Saviano tobaccoless herbal cigarettes to puff on before they actually filmed the scene.

"The boys were so professional," says the producer. "Even though they never smoked before, neither one of them coughed."

Fred said later of his first experience with smoking,

"Josh and I were saying, 'This is cool, we're going to smoke in this scene.' But then we tried it, and it was *really* gross!"

While that scene left a bad taste in Fred's mouth, there was another scene that was also not on his favorite list. The dream sequence where he had to drop down onto his teacher's desk in his underwear was "*so* embarrassing," winces Fred. "It's my least favorite thing to do." In another episode Fred had to cry on cue.

As *The Wonder Years* continues to burn up the airwaves, Fred finds himself with less time to call his own. In spite of his grueling schedule, however, Fred manages to find time for everything. For three hours a day, he studies his schoolwork on the set with a tutor. He rehearses the show all week, doing his homework between rehearsals. Sometimes he must be on the set six days a week.

The interesting thing about Fred is that he is a perfectionist. While his parents would be satisfied if he received all Bs in his subjects, Fred studies hard enough to achieve almost straight As.

"Once I failed a science quiz," he says. "But I studied extra-hard, and by the end of the year, I got an A in the class. Science is now my favorite subject."

On the set of the show, Fred keeps the rest of the cast going with his energy and undying zest. Josh Saviano, who plays Kevin's buddy Paul Pfeiffer, describes Fred as "real funny. He comes up with the weirdest things. Just out of the blue, he makes the whole set crack up, and then he goes right back to normal like nothing ever happened."

After working nonstop on the show and keeping up with schoolwork, most kids would want to rest on weekends or in their spare time. But not Fred.

He seems to be in perpetual motion—even when he doesn't have to be. He takes dancing lessons and practices the piano during his free time.

Fred believes in applying himself one hundred percent and always does his absolute best. Even though studying for school tests *and* memorizing his lines for the show may sometimes get tiring, he makes sure he has enough time for both.

Fred has come up with a very unique way of learning his part. "I look at the script and the scenes," he explains. "Then I put my hand over the script and move down the page. When I see someone else's line, I move down. And then when it comes to my line, I keep my hand over it. I say the line and pick up my hand to see if it's right. I just keep doing that until I learn my entire part."

When Fred finishes filming an episode and the show is ready to be aired, he will sometimes watch it. "I'm very critical of myself," he says. "I always say, 'I should have done this better,' or 'I didn't do that.' But mostly I just sit back and enjoy the show like everyone else."

Fred has become such a natural and instinctive actor, he knows when he has done something wrong in a scene before the director has a chance to tell him.

Because the voice of actor Daniel Stern plays the older Kevin and narrates much of the show, Fred's body language and facial expressions are very important to the scenes of the show. In one scene where Kevin wakes up from a nightmare in a cold sweat, Fred stopped the action and said to the director, "I know I moved my head too fast on that one." It took three takes before both Fred and the director were satisfied.

Fred has his movements down perfectly, and he is very effective in his role. The audience feels everything his character goes through each week—and that can be fully credited to Fred's fine abilities as an actor.

For many viewers *The Wonder Years* is the most compelling and meaningful show on television. In 1989 it won the Emmy Award for the best show of the year, and it was also honored at the Golden Globe Awards.

Referring to the unbelievable success of *The Wonder Years,* Fred says, "I think it's reached so many people because for young kids it's a kids' show about kids in the 1960s. And for adults it brings back memories of that time. I've had a lot of adults come up to me and say, 'That episode where you were calling that girl— that was me.' This show is so different from any other show on TV," adds Fred, "that I wouldn't mind doing it for a long, long time."

· 7 ·

MEET FRED'S
TV FAMILY

Fred Savage knows the importance of ensemble acting. Even though most of *The Wonder Years* centers on him, he admits he'd be nowhere without the rest of the cast. All the actors have described their experience with the show as the best time they've ever had. No one demands the spotlight, and that is very important.

The cast of *The Wonder Years* is a close-knit group, and the atmosphere on the set is a happy one. Some of the cast members have become so friendly that when the cameras stop rolling, they see each other outside of work.

Fred's closest friend on and off the set of the show is New Jersey–born Josh Saviano, who plays Paul Pfeiffer. Fred and Josh have a lot in common, both personally and professionally.

Like Fred, Josh became an actor on impulse. At age five he and his mother took a neighborhood actor friend to Manhattan to see his manager. On the spur of the moment, Josh asked if he could see the manager, too. He gave a reading and was signed but didn't get his first professional acting job until one year later when he was six years old. Like Fred, Josh's first acting job was in a commercial, and he did several spots for products like Aim toothpaste and Campbell's soup.

Josh then won roles in movies but didn't have the same luck Fred had. Josh did a voice-over in an unreleased film called *That's Adequate* and appeared only briefly in Woody Allen's *Radio Days*. "I started out in a very large role as one of the kids," he says. "But my part ended up on the cutting-room floor." He also appeared with Mark Hamill on Broadway in a play titled *The Nerd*.

Josh feels very fortunate to have won the steady part of Paul in *The Wonder Years*. Playing Kevin's best friend, he dons glasses and portrays a character completely different from his own personality.

Fred describes Josh as "a real pro. He is nothing like Paul. In real life Josh doesn't wear glasses and is a normal, friendly guy. We play video games all the time. We play all kinds of sports together, and he also collects baseball cards."

Of the four teens on the show, only Fred and Josh, who are the same age, go to school on the set. Jason Hervey and Danica McKellar are enrolled in local public schools.

Jason Hervey, who plays the role of Wayne Arnold, has been acting all his life. He began at age four and has worked nonstop. His first job was in a ketchup commercial, and at age seven he appeared in a Levi's jeans commercial that won the Clio award.

At age twelve Jason was teaching jazz and pop dancing, and some of his students were fellow acting friends. "I taught River Phoenix, his sister Rainbow, and his brother Leaf to breakdance," smiles Jason, who is close friends with teen stars Kirk Cameron, Alyssa Milano, and Scott Grimes.

Jason's TV credits include guest-starring roles on *Trapper John, M.D.; The Two of Us; The Love Boat; Taxi; Alice; Punky Brewster; Simon and Simon; Together We Stand;* and *A Year in the Life.* He was a series regular on *Fast Times at Ridgemont High* and the last season of *Diff'rent Strokes.*

In addition, Jason's feature-film roles include *Pee-Wee's Big Adventure, Back to the Future, Police Academy II, The Buddy System, Meatballs II, The Monster Squad,* and the young Rodney Dangerfield in *Back to School.*

Jason recently added a new project to his credit.

When he's not working on *The Wonder Years,* he is the host of the TV show *Wide World of Kids,* a syndicated show for teens that is educational and entertaining. The show goes on movie locations and profiles young people who have done out-of-the-ordinary things.

On *The Wonder Years* Jason's character is a real bully to younger brother Kevin. But he says of the TV role he plays so convincingly, "I'm so far from being Wayne Arnold that it's not even funny. I'm really sensitive." In real life Jason has an older brother, so he knows what it feels like to be teased.

When Fred describes working with Jason, he confides, "The thing I like best about him is that he's really outgoing—and wild! He tells me all about the wild things he and his friends do on the weekends. He always makes me laugh."

Although it is Jason who is known as the practical joker on the set, Fred has played a joke or two on his fellow castmate. One time he snuck into Jason's dressing room and switched the bar of soap with a trick one that turns your hands and face black when you wash with it. It probably beat any trick Jason played on Fred.

Pretty Danica McKellar was originally signed to play Winnie Cooper only in the pilot of *The Wonder Years,* but the producers liked her so much they decided to keep her on as a series regular.

Danica began acting when she was nine years old.

She had been a professional dancer and was encouraged to give acting a try. At first Danica turned down the idea, saying, "I think I'd be really embarrassed." But one year later she told her mother that she wanted to try it. Both Danica and her sister Crystal were signed by an agency, and Danica began auditioning and winning roles on TV.

The McKellar sisters were both asked to read for the role of Winnie in *The Wonder Years*. Since Fred was the first actor cast for the show, he read with all the people auditioning so that the producers could study the chemistry between Fred and each actor.

Danica and Crystal both read well and were both final choices for the part. Their first audition was on a Thursday, and on Friday they were called back to read again.

The producers thought it was interesting that two sisters were trying out for the same part, and they really couldn't decide between the two. Finally they chose Danica because the character of Winnie was older, and Danica is two years older than Crystal.

Like Winnie, Danica is very sweet and quiet. She is serious about her schoolwork; she has won honors and awards for her proficiency in math and French, and she plans to go to college. She loves it when people talk to her about the show, and she gets along great with costars Fred and Josh. Although she is one year older than the boys, they seem to share many interests.

Fred says of Danica, "She's a great dancer and a whiz at video games."

Off-screen Danica loves to ski and swim and is currently taking synchronized swimming lessons. She is an avid collector of Garfield books and stuffed animals. Her mom comments, "About four years ago I was given a small Garfield toy as a gift. Danica fell in love with it and has been collecting them ever since. She gets Garfield toys and books for every holiday, and people give them to her as gifts all year round."

Danica also developed a passion for growing plants and persuaded her mother to let her design and plant a walkway and garden at their house in Los Angeles. Like her on-screen costar Fred, Danica is also an on-the-go teen who never sits still for very long.

Karen Arnold is the only character on *The Wonder Years* who is affected by the times. As Kevin's older hippie sister, actress Olivia d'Abo was born a true child of the 1960s. Olivia is the only daughter of Michael d'Abo, former lead singer of the classic rock band, Manfred Mann. Her mother, Maggie London d'Abo, was a top model in London for ten years and had feature roles in two cult-classic 1960s films, *A Hard Day's Night* with the Beatles and *2001: A Space Odyssey*.

Olivia, born in London, England, moved with her mother and older brother to Los Angeles, California, after her parents divorced. At thirteen she appeared in commercials and won roles in feature films *Bolero*,

Conan the Destroyer, and *A Dream to Believe.* She also guest-starred on the TV shows *Growing Pains, Simon and Simon, The Bronx Zoo,* and *Tour of Duty.*

Olivia graduated from high school two years ago and leads an incredibly full life when she is not concentrating on her flourishing acting career. She enjoys swimming, horseback riding, and skiing. But her number-one love is music, and her favorite pastime is composing and writing song lyrics.

Since the show's time period has progressed from the late 1960s into the early 1970s this past year, Olivia's character has taken her antiwar activism to college. She loves playing Karen because, she says, "It's the most challenging role I've ever portrayed. I think it's a good vehicle because people see me as an actress. I'm definitely not the character they see on the show."

Fred also has a great relationship with his TV parents, Dan Lauria and Alley Mills. When playing the role of Fred's TV dad, Jack Arnold, Dan lives out an early dream. Born in Brooklyn, New York, and raised in Lindenhurst, Long Island, Dan grew up loving all the old black-and-white movies starring James Cagney and other Hollywood legends. He knew from an early age that he wanted to become an actor, but he first became involved with sports in high school and college.

In the early 1970s he rediscovered his love for acting. He wrote and performed in many off-Broadway plays and made his TV debut on the soap opera

Love of Life. It was the first in a long line of acting jobs for Dan in both TV and movies.

Fred Savage and his TV mom, Alley Mills, both hail from the area surrounding Chicago, Illinois. Alley is a veteran TV actress, having starred as a regular in the short-lived series *The Associates* opposite Martin Short, and as a guest on the shows *Moonlighting*, *Lou Grant*, and *Hill Street Blues*.

Alley lives in California and enjoys camping in the mountains and hunting for antiques for her small New England–style home.

The Wonder Years stars are a very special group who light up the small screen week after week. All the cast members know they can count on each other. They understand and respect one another, and they are more than just coworkers on a television show.

Though Fred is the one who has achieved stardom, the others do not resent his popularity and success. For the most part these actors were all unknowns before the series tossed them into the limelight of fame. They realize that the entire cast has made this show the hit it has become. Fred's sensitive portrayal of Kevin Arnold is part of the reason for the overwhelming success of the series, but this success has made all of the cast members well known. *The Wonder Years* is definitely a group effort all the way.

Fred is grateful to be working with such a talented and great group of people. The daily support he gets from Josh, Jason, Danica, Olivia, and his on-screen parents, Dan Lauria and Alley Mills, is incredible. These people have become a second family to Fred, and there will always be a special place in his life for them.

Fred Savage:
Hollywood's boy
wonder.
(Photo by Scott Downie/
Celebrity Photo)

Fred's family has been beside him every step of the way. The Savages are (left to right) Joanne, Fred, Lew, (front) Ben, and Kala.

(Photo by John Paschal/
Celebrity Photo)

Fred, dressed casually in a loose-fitting, oversize shirt, loves his new California life-style.

(Photo by Scott Downie/ Celebrity Photo)

The cast of *The Wonder Years* at the 41st Annual Emmy Awards. Left to right: Jason Hervey, Fred, Olivia d'Abo, Danica McKellar, Ally Mills, Josh Saviano, and Dan Lauria.

(Photo by John Paschal/ Celebrity Photo)

Fred and his TV parents, Dan Lauria and Ally Mills, were on hand to accept the Golden Globe award for *The Wonder Years*.

(Photo by Scott Downie/ Celebrity Photo)

Fred looks great in a tuxedo, but he is more comfortable in jeans and sporty shirts.

"I owe all my success to my mom," says Fred. "I couldn't have done any of this without her."

Comic Relief

Fred has been
applauded for his
spunkiness, his
naturalness and his flair
for handling his role on
The Wonder Years. Here
he is at Comic Relief III,
a show to benefit
America's homeless.

(Photo by Scott Downie/
Celebrity Photo)

Fred gives his younger brother, Ben, a lift at a party held at the Disney Studios.

(Photo by Janet Gough/ Celebrity Photo)

Fred and his TV brother, Jason Hervey, at the 15th Annual People's Choice Awards.

(Photo by Smeal/Galella Ltd.)

An avid baseball fan, Fred participated in this Los Angeles Dodgers all-star charity game at Dodger Stadium in Anaheim, California.

(Photo by Smeal/Galella Ltd.)

At the 15th Annual
People's Choice
Awards, Fred presented
the Favorite Young
Television Performer
award to Kirk Cameron
of *Growing Pains*.

(Photo by Smeal/Galella Ltd.)

All-American Fred poses with a teddy bear at the 57th Annual Hollywood Christmas Parade.
(Photo by Scott Downie/ Celebrity Photo)

Fred and his *Wonder Years* costar and onscreen love interest, Danica McKellar.
(Photo courtesy of Capital Cities/ ABC, Inc.)

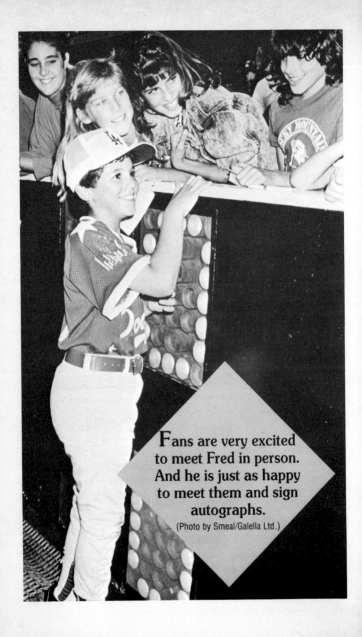

Fans are very excited to meet Fred in person. And he is just as happy to meet them and sign autographs.

(Photo by Smeal/Galella Ltd.)

Fred and Jenny Lewis,
his costar in *The
Wizard*, arrive at the
movie's premiere at the
Cineplex Odeon in
Universal City,
California.

(Photo by Smeal/Galella Ltd.)

Fred is keeping a level
head about his show-
business career. "I don't
want to get a big head,"
he says, "because then
people will stop liking
me."

·8·

GIRLS AND DATING

When Fred Savage is interviewed, one of the questions he is usually asked is, "What kind of girl do you like?" At only fourteen years old, Fred hasn't had too much experience with dating, but that doesn't stop him from talking about his dream girl.

"I like someone I can talk to," he says. "I like girls who are nice and pretty, not too wild but not too shy either."

When Fred started acting, his younger sister was

nervous about bringing her friends home. There had been a lot of stories floating around Hollywood about teenage stars. Sometimes kids would pose as "friends" of the family just to get close to the "star."

This has never happened to the Savage family because they were extra-careful. Kala in particular wanted to be sure that her friends were honest—that they didn't want to hang out with her just because her brother was on TV.

Fred has always been a friendly guy. Whenever he meets someone, he greets them with a smile and a big hello. But Kala kept her famous brother away from her friends.

"When she brings home friends, I'll try to say hi to them," says Fred with an innocent grin. "But she won't let me talk to them."

When it comes to dating, Fred can't really say exactly what kind of person the girl he takes out should be. He likes girls who are down-to-earth and caring, girls who are natural, who say what they feel and are candid about their emotions. Fred demands honesty and sincerity above everything else; he doesn't like someone who is phony or stuck-up. His favorite kind of girl is someone who appreciates him as a person and not just as a star.

One friend he was very close to back home in Glencoe, Illinois, was a girl named Abra Dresher. "My dad went to high school with her mom," explains Fred. "And then my mom and her mom became really good friends. So we grew up together. We lived in the same neighborhood, and I don't think a day went by when I was young that I didn't see Abra."

Fred liked being around Abra because she shared his interests in music and sports. Like Fred, she also loved going to the movies, and they would often stop by McDonald's for a quick bite to eat before seeing the matinee.

With Abra, Fred felt he could talk about everything. In some ways Abra knew more about Fred than he knew about himself. Whatever he wanted to talk to her about, whether it was his acting career or a problem he was having with a subject in school, she'd listen and help in whatever way she could.

When Fred won his role on *The Wonder Years* and had to live in Los Angeles for months at a time, he missed Abra. His mom thought it would be great to have Abra fly to the West Coast and stay with them for a while. During the first season of *The Wonder Years*, Fred and Abra appeared to be dating. But Fred told reporters, "Abra came out to L.A. to visit me. It was really nice, but we're not going steady. I've just known her all my life. We like going to the movies and the mall."

When Abra went back home, Fred stayed on in Los Angeles. He still sees her when he goes home to Glencoe, and they are still very good friends.

As one of the brightest and busiest teen stars in Hollywood, Fred doesn't have time right now to devote to dating. For Fred it's something he looks forward to in the years ahead. He's the kind of guy who feels it's necessary to give most of his time to the girl of his dreams. Being away for months at a time working on a movie wouldn't be fair to her.

As Fred begins his teenage years, finding the right girl is very much in his thoughts. As far as looks go, Fred doesn't have a favorite type. She could be tall, short, blond, brunette—it really doesn't matter as long as they have fun together.

More important to Fred is her personality. She must be friendly and have a good sense of humor. Being an actor in a comedy show, Fred loves to laugh and claims he cracks up at everything including, "The why-did-the-chicken-cross-the-road joke," he says. Fred likes being around people who are ready to have fun and good times.

Fred is outgoing and fun loving, and he looks for the same qualities in the friends he chooses and in a possible girlfriend. He is not really into going to dance clubs or to parties, but he wouldn't disappoint his girlfriend if she wanted to do those things.

Anyone who knows Fred knows that he is a warm, affectionate young man. He is very romantic, and he's not afraid to show his feelings to the people he loves.

Fred was raised in a very loving environment. His parents have provided their children with a stable home life and have shown them the importance of family. As his dad says, "The family is our top priority.

Whatever comes up, we stay together. If Fred had to go to Timbuktu for a movie, we'd all go with him." Because Fred is so close to his parents and younger siblings, he'll often bring a girl home first to meet the Savage clan.

Fred admits that both his mother and sister have, in some way, affected his choice of girls. Joanne and her daughter Kala are very independent individuals, and Fred has come to respect that quality in women. He honestly doesn't know if he could handle dating a girl who didn't have her own interests and pursuits.

Fred's basic idea of a date is a day or night when a guy and a girl go out and get to know each other. When a girl is with Fred, she is the very center of his attention.

Fred used to think going to the mall was a lot of fun. For a long time it was his idea of the perfect date. Now he prefers going to a restaurant, a movie, and maybe for a quiet walk on the beach or around his neighborhood. Fred is very active, and while there are times when he just likes talking, he also enjoys indulging in sports or playing video games.

Fred is also very spontaneous. Sometimes he doesn't plan a date ahead of time but will do something completely on the spur of the moment. The only time Fred believes in making plans in advance is for things like birthday parties. Otherwise, he doesn't mind going out on very short notice—that is, if he doesn't have to work.

Fred Savage is very much in demand. His sudden surge in popularity came quickly, and he knows that he should accept it and enjoy it. He is completely immersed in his acting career, and, it is obvious how much he loves what he is doing.

Fred is certainly too young to think about marriage but admits to having considered the subject. Someday he'd like to settle down and start a family, but he adds, "I have plenty of time for all that. I'm kind of enjoying acting and everything that's going on in my life right now!"

·9·

THE SAVAGE KIDS IN
LITTLE MONSTERS

When Fred Savage read the script for an offbeat movie about "little monsters," he found it interesting. It was different from any other film he had ever done, and he decided he wanted to play the role of Brian Stevenson.

On paper *Little Monsters* seemed promising. It mixed comedy, adventure, and fantasy and had some pretty impressive stunts and special effects. Fred was especially excited to be doing some "flying" in the movie, something he refers to as "a lifetime dream come true."

The only thing he wasn't too happy about was a special harness that had to be attached to his body. "I didn't care for that," he says. "But the flying part was really fun. There's one part in the movie where I have to soar over this real deep drop that goes down about fifteen feet. That was kind of scary. But all in all, I had a great time!"

When Fred signed on to be one of the stars of *Little Monsters,* the producers were looking for the perfect actor to play his younger brother. They wanted someone just like Fred, a smaller version of the talented boy wonder. The only other young actor in Hollywood who could fill that order was Fred's little brother Ben. He showed up at the auditions, read for the role, and won it.

Little Monsters marked the first time Fred Savage, his brother Ben, *and* younger sister Kala appeared together in a movie. The talented Savage kids talked of working together someday but never thought it would be so soon.

Fred's dad in *Little Monsters* was played by Daniel Stern, the actor who does the voice-overs of the adult Kevin Arnold in each episode of *The Wonder Years*.

Fred was scheduled to begin filming the movie during his hiatus from *The Wonder Years*. In May 1989 he wrapped all the episodes for the season and packed his suitcase to go to the film's location. Fred's family traveled with him to the production's headquarters in Wilmington, North Carolina, where they stayed until the movie was completed.

In the past his brother and sister used to tag along for the fun of watching Fred work on a movie, but now things were different. Ben's role in the movie was just as important as Fred's. And Kala was going to portray one of the "little monsters." This movie was going to be a *real* Savage family project.

Fred's mother, Joanne, never expected all three of her children to become actors. She had an entirely different life planned for herself and her family. "I was planning to work with my husband in his business, retire someday in Florida, and play bridge and tennis," she says. "At home I drove car pools and made dinner every night. Then this show-biz thing expanded and took over more and more of our lives."

Ben became interested in acting after watching Fred on the big and small screens. Like his older brother, he started auditioning and winning roles in television commercials. "Ben was so proud to be on TV like his big brother," says Lew Savage. "But somehow there's a difference. When Fred started, we didn't expect this. When he did his first commercial, we were unbelievably overjoyed. Fred has had the privilege of being the pioneer in the family. I just hope the other two can enjoy themselves as much as he did, instead of looking for the next mountain to conquer. When Ben did his first commercial, I said, 'Wow, Ben, you're on TV.' And he looked at me and said, 'When will I be in a movie?'"

Curly-haired, adorable Ben Savage is extremely ambitious. He wants to do it all just like Fred. Yet in some ways Ben is more easygoing than his big brother.

Joanne says, "I don't have too many worries with Ben. You could throw him against a wall, and he'd just bounce off and keep going. He's bright, social, and winsome."

Ben was five years old when he started appearing in a string of television commercials for Osco Drugs, Wheaties, Chloraseptic, McDonald's, and Cracker Jacks. He was eight when he won the starring role of Eric in *Little Monsters* opposite Fred. Ben was proud of the fact that for his motion-picture debut, he was playing a character older than himself.

"Eric is nine years old, and I'm eight," he said. He also pointed out that, unlike himself, the character he plays is "mostly scared of things. He's real scared of monsters."

The story of *Little Monsters* begins as every child's nightmare with the question, Are there monsters under my bed? Young Eric Stevenson thinks there are, and he may be right. His older brother Brian (played by Fred) doesn't believe in monsters but realizes that something strange is going on.

In their home there is evidence of mischievous doings—a container full of melted ice cream is left on the kitchen counter all night, and a bicycle left in the driveway is crushed by Dad's car. Brian is blamed for both incidents, so he sets out to find the real culprit.

He is forced to take matters into his own hands.

Brian switches bedrooms with Eric and constructs an elaborate homemade trap in order to capture the "monster under the bed."

The trap is sprung, and Brian comes face-to-face with Maurice (Howie Mandel), a monster who is totally hip, ultracool, and single-handedly responsible for all the recent mayhem in the house. Without realizing it Brian begins the adventure of his life.

He helps Maurice escape back under his bed. The following night Maurice invites Brian to visit his world, where every kid's fantasy comes true. In his world there are no rules, no homework, plenty of games, and an endless supply of junk food.

After three visits to the underworld, Brian finds it isn't all fun and games. The place is ruled by a mysterious entity known as Boy, whose sinister bodyguard, Snik, takes an immediate dislike to Brian.

When Eric is kidnapped and Brian is told he knows too much and must become one of the little monsters, things take a sudden turn. Brian convinces his friends Todd (William Murray Weiss) and Kiersten (Amber Barretto) to join him on his search-and-rescue mission.

Fred's sister, Kala, who appears as one of the little monsters in the movie, is unrecognizable because of all the makeup that had to be applied to her face. Kala, who is also a regular on the daytime soap opera *Santa Barbara,* isn't really sure she wants to be an actress all her life. She's had a lot of fun portraying different roles but doesn't know yet if acting will remain her career choice in the future.

"Despite Kala's success, she isn't as set on acting as Fred," contends Joanne. "If she has certain plans and there's an audition, she sometimes doesn't want to give up that plan to go."

While the Savage brothers are energetic and outgoing, Kala doesn't feel completely comfortable being in the spotlight. "She's the sweetest of the sweet," smiles her mother. "She's quieter than the boys, which used to worry me. It's hard being sandwiched between two live wires like Fred and Ben."

With three little actors under one roof, is there ever any competition between them? Fred says, "No. We aren't competitive. We're just like regular brothers and sisters. We're not *The Brady Bunch*. We fight, but then we always make up. We're just ourselves."

Kala adds, "We don't have fights too much except over what's on TV and who gets to hold the remote control. I steal Fred's shampoo a lot, and that gets him mad."

The older Savage kids, Fred and Kala, like to tease their little brother Ben. "We get really frustrated with Ben and his karate," moans Kala. "Yeah, he got a yellow belt, and he thinks he's a Bruce Lee ninja!" reports Fred.

He does admit there are times when "I get sent to my room for fighting with my brother and sister or mouthing off to my parents. But that doesn't happen too much. We're a close family."

Throughout the filming of *Little Monsters*, the Savage kids had a good time between takes. Once the cameras started to roll, they were completely professional. All three kids received nothing but praise from the people they worked with on the set of *Little Monsters*. Special-effects engineer Robert Short said, "Both Fred and Ben are exquisite actors. Kala had to sit for hours to have a head cast made for her. All of the kids were really patient and very high-energy!"

One of the producers said of Fred and his fine acting job in the film, "He's the best actor in his age group in this country!"

The *Little Monsters* experience was a good one for Fred. He was pleasantly surprised by his brother's fantastic acting abilities. "It was fun working with my brother for the first time," says Fred enthusiastically. "It was fun watching him act. He was really good."

And little Ben had a lot of fun in his first movie acting opposite Fred. In fact, he gives his brother credit for making this movie memorable. "Being with Fred on the set was fun because I know him a lot," offers Ben, smiling widely.

Ben went from his role in *Little Monsters* to the part of Judd Hirsch's young son Matthew in the TV series *Dear John*. The producers of the show were looking for an actor with the appeal Fred has on *The Wonder Years* and decided Ben fit that description.

With all the work the Savage kids are doing, they have been taught by their parents not to let it overpower their lives. The love among the Savage family reigns above everything. They've gotten through the good and bad times because they care so much for each other. "If a parent is crazy for kids, as we are, then those kids hear it loud and clear," says Fred's dad. "I think a parent's joy is infinite. And if you don't enjoy the journey, it really isn't worth it. Everything that has happened has been fun for us."

While Fred and his family have good memories of *Little Monsters,* it was, unfortunately, a movie plagued with problems. They began when the set mysteriously caught fire in the middle of the night. Luckily no one was hurt, but some costumes and props did go up in smoke.

Then there were releasing problems. Sometimes a movie gets lost in the shuffle of big-name pictures. It is released in a few theaters, receives mixed reviews, and usually disappears more quickly than it appeared. *Little Monsters* was to suffer such a fate. It wasn't given the right publicity or promotion to keep it in the minds of the public. However, it's been given a second chance. MGM/UA Home Video released a videotape of *Little Monsters* in March 1990, hoping it would find the audience it deserves in the video market.

Immediately after finishing the movie, Fred thought he would be able to go back home to Glencoe before he had to return to the set of *The Wonder Years.* There was still a little over four weeks left of the summer before shooting for the new season began in late July.

But when you're as hot as Fred, there's no time for a vacation. Ken Topolsky, who produced the 1989–90 season of *The Wonder Years*, was also the producer, along with David Chisholm, of a movie titled *The Wizard*. Topolsky, who cites Chisholm and Fred Savage as two of his best friends, wanted his young series star to play the role of Corey in the movie.

Fred agreed to do the film, and less than one week later, the Savage family traveled from North Carolina, where *Little Monsters* was filmed, to Las Vegas, Nevada, the primary location of *The Wizard*.

·10·

FRED'S JOURNEY TO SUCCESS

"*The Wizard* is a different role for me," says Fred Savage. "I'm pretty aggressive in it. I do my own thing, make up my own mind, and don't listen to my dad or brother at all. I think it will be a good movie and that kids will really like it. It has everything—action, video games, and lots of comedy."

Fred was right on target. *The Wizard* was on an extremely tight production schedule because Fred had to wrap up filming so he could begin the new season of *The Wonder Years*. Everything had to run smoothly and did. *The Wizard* was a successful film, and the positive atmosphere on the set probably contributed to the end result.

"We were very lucky to get Fred," says Ken Topolsky, one of the film's producers. "He was our first choice for the part of Corey. Fred is very much in demand. We had to have all his scenes finished by the twenty-sixth before we lost him."

Todd Holland, who made his directorial debut on this movie, says, "We were constantly under the gun: high pressure, long hours, tough locations. I've worked with some great people before, but this crew was amazing. Talented, tireless, and possessed of a life-saving sense of humor!"

The producers handpicked Holland, who was an award-winning short-subject director. A graduate of the UCLA Film and Television School, Holland wrote, produced, and directed the live-action animated short film, *Chicken Thing*, which won twenty international awards, including the prestigious CINE Award. *The Wizard* was the kind of movie he always dreamed of doing.

"I was raised on kid adventure movies," he says. "*The Wizard* possessed all of that energy but also offered an emotional richness that seemed unique for this genre. But I probably couldn't have picked a more difficult first feature: a road movie with a very short prep, dozens of locations, literally hundreds of kids, video playback—all on a nearly impossible schedule. But the story had real heart, and I think the film we've made will appeal to all ages."

The crew on this movie was chosen with special care because of the pace they would have to be working. People specializing in wardrobe and transportation came from *The Wonder Years*. Camera, grip, and electric crews as well as assistant directors had all worked with Holland on HBO's *Vietnam War Story*. The idea of "family" would extend far beyond the crew.

The cast also had relatives and friends on the set. With Fred's family present and the families of other cast members in attendance, the set of *The Wizard* felt like a summer camp. Before each take the assistant director had to calm down the kids, who would often run around playing tag, baseball, or Frisbee. Some went on searches for lizards and snakes in the hot desert of Nevada, and one Sunday afternoon most of the cast and crew went white-water rafting on the Truckee River. Says Topolsky with a smile, "It was more fun than a movie is supposed to be."

Nothing was overlooked if it was to make this production more enjoyable. Someone discovered that Fred, Chisholm, and a few crew members had birthdays during the month of July. On each birthday a cake was brought out, and their special days were celebrated right there on the set.

In the movie Fred plays Corey Woods, a wily charmer whose happy family life has disintegrated over the last few years. His father, Sam (Beau Bridges), has divorced his stepmother, Christine (Wendy Phillips), and is now out of touch with his three sons. Corey's older brother, Nick (Christian Slater), is rebellious, and his younger half brother, Jimmy (Luke Edwards), has become deeply withdrawn and has stopped talking.

Corey tries to help Jimmy break out of his shell. The boy expresses an interest in going to California and playing complicated video games. So Corey decides to run away with him to Los Angeles and enter him in the National Video Championship. Along the way Corey takes on a partner and romantic counterpart when Haley (Jenny Lewis), a thirteen-year-old video-game hustler, joins them.

The Wizard is about a boy's love for his brother, but also about a father and his relationship with his sons. It isn't until Corey leaves with Jimmy that Sam realizes what has happened to his family. Nick and Sam set out to find the youngsters and ultimately father and sons are brought together again.

Writer-producer David Chisholm was inspired to write *The Wizard*. "A neighbor's son had extreme trouble relating to other people and also suffered from poor hand-eye coordination," he says. "The father bought the boy several home video games and worked with him on playing them in hope of drawing him out. The result was that he showed great interest in the games, and his hand-eye coordination dramatically improved."

Chisholm believes the games are about reaching goals. "They present obstacles and choices wrapped in a story line that are themselves little journeys at which the player alone either fails or succeeds. Like the games, the journey the kids take in the movie is theirs alone, and they fail or succeed based upon their choices."

The Wizard began filming on June 7, 1989, and completed principal photography on July 28. Locations during the first two weeks included the rural Nevada cities of Minden, Gardnerville, Fallon, Hazen, Dayton, and Lake Tahoe. Filming resumed for two weeks in and around the Reno area, including such locations as the Bally's casino, the Peppermill and Riverboat casinos, and Pyramid Lake. The final weeks of filming took place at various rural Southern California locations, including Acton, Valencia, and Palm Desert.

The numerous locations gave the movie a realistic, wide-open feel. There were only a few problems moving the cast and crew from one set to another.

The film had virtually no time for advance preparation. That meant they shot the scenes from day to day without knowing what the next set was going to look like until they were on it ready to film. "Our art department was usually one location ahead of us on any given day," says Holland. "We ended up seeing a finished set for the first time as we walked in to start shooting."

Although it did get nerve-racking acting under this kind of pressure, the worst day for the cast and crew was the day they shot their scenes in Reno. When the cast and director Holland arrived ten minutes before the crew, no one had seen the set before. In just half a day the lighting had to be quickly adjusted, and all the scenes had to be finished to stay on schedule. They were lucky that the city of Reno was very cooperative with the production company.

They shut the main street down from eight p.m. until two a.m. on a Friday night, when traffic was heavy, just to accommodate the filming. The best part of the filming for Fred was inside the casinos. He was mesmerized by all the people who were standing in front of slot machines gambling.

Fred described working at all the locations in Nevada as, "Great! I'd never been to that part of the country before. I'd never seen real deserts and casinos. They were unbelievable. I had to try gambling just once. I won money. I told my mom what numbers to play, and she won."

Producer Ken Topolsky said of his energetic, self-assured star, "There's not another young actor like Fred. He's a complete natural, and even at his young age he makes each character he plays unique, and each take is different. Just as important, he's a warm-hearted, sensitive person, and his manner and presence encourage film crews to work extra-hard because they get so attached to him."

Even though Fred was there to work, he didn't let a day go by without having some good old-fashioned fun and getting to know his coworkers. When Holland remembers the days of filming *The Wizard*, he says, "Our cast was amazing. Beau, Christian, Wendy, Will, and Sam were all good people, talented and gracious. And the only hard part about working with Fred, Jenny, and Luke was finding them."

The three young stars of the movie were usually off playing sports or just talking. The director said about Luke Edwards, his youngest star, "The joy with Luke was, if we needed him and couldn't find him, we just had to locate the nearest video game, because that's exactly where he'd be."

The Wizard was one of the first movies Luke Edwards appeared in. He is the extraordinary young actor in the first half of the TV drama *I Know My First Name Is Steven*. Fred says of Luke, "He is very good and will be very successful real soon."

Luke enjoyed working with Fred. The boys often talked about acting. "I learned a lot from Fred," says Luke. "He had a lot to tell me about acting. He's been in the business since he was six years old."

Fred also got along well with Jenny Lewis, one of the few girls in the cast. Jenny says about Fred, "He is so quick! He's one of the smartest and funniest actors I've ever met! It was wonderful to be working on a set with people my own age. There was always some kind of game going on. Every day at lunch we'd play either baseball, basketball, volleyball, or Frisbee."

When it was time for this trio of teenagers to go to their marks and film their scenes, they were fully prepared. "Fred would blow you away with his focus and ability," says Holland. "And Jenny was always the consummate professional and a joy to work with. As for Luke, well, he's a terrific little actor."

What about that kissing scene between Fred and Jenny? Did Fred find it as difficult to do as his kiss with Danica McKellar on *The Wonder Years*? "Yes, it's always difficult because there are so many people watching," he sighs.

Jenny agrees. "Fred and I would rehearse the scene without the kiss because we were both kind of nervous," she says. "Then when we filmed it, we kissed. It turned out kind of funny. It's not the most romantic kiss you'll ever see. After we filmed it, I felt embarrassed. All the crew members clapped or laughed or cheered."

Fred describes his role in *The Wizard* as "a little bit of a hustler, which I've never done before. I get to experiment a lot in this movie."

Fred sees his character's reasoning for abducting his younger brother and taking him to California. "Jimmy never got to do anything he wanted to do," explains Fred. "When he spoke the word 'California,' a light went off in Corey's head, and he knew that he had to take Jimmy there to give him a taste of freedom."

Would Fred do the same for his own younger brother, Ben? "No way," he laughs. "I wouldn't survive it. He wouldn't survive it."

During the filming of *The Wizard*, Fred suffered only one setback when he came down with a slight case of pneumonia. It almost looked as if production would have to be delayed, but he recovered and was back to work after a short rest.

The Wizard was edited just as quickly as it was filmed. On December 15, 1989, the movie was released in time for the Christmas movie rush. It was billed as a good family picture, the kind parents and kids could go see together. Everyone was proud of the movie. Even Beau Bridges said, "I did this film because I wanted something I could take my kids to see."

Fred worked straight through the summer of 1989 and didn't have much time off in the fall of that year either. When school began in September, Fred hit the books. He was worried his grades would fall because of the work schedule, so he studied extra-hard. In fact, his dad wouldn't allow Fred to travel anywhere to promote his two movies. Lew didn't want his son to take any extra time away from his studies.

Between his schoolwork and memorizing his *Wonder Years* role, Fred spent the second half of 1989 working. But he has no regrets. The year was a very productive one for him, and he says he'd do it all over again exactly the same way. "There's only one downside to all this," says Fred. "And that would be that I'm away from my friends a lot."

LIFE WITH FRED

In his career so far, Fred Savage has played many different roles. His fans have seen him as 1960s kid Kevin Arnold on *The Wonder Years*, a boy trying to deal with the death of his father in *The Boy Who Could Fly*, an adult trapped inside a boy's body in *Vice Versa*, and a regular kid being read a story by his grandfather in *The Princess Bride*.

Fred is so convincing in each of these diversified roles that it is difficult to determine what Fred the person is really like. Is he like someone you know? Is he different from the star you see acting in movies and television?

Those who are closest to Fred speak of his modesty and down-to-earth personality. Fred isn't the type to let media name tags like "star" bother him. He doesn't consider himself to be a star, despite the fact that he is on top right now. Yet, while Fred may be wary about the term, there's no denying that *The Wonder Years* and his movies, especially *The Wizard,* have made him a media personality. Actually, the more successful Fred has become, the more he has projected naturalness and self-confidence.

Fred Savage has been described by his adult co-workers as a "nice kid." No one seems to mind being with Fred for hours at a time. On the set he is a true professional. He'll redo his scenes countless times until the director says, "Cut! That's a print." And he'll do them willingly because he is a perfectionist. Fred won't let anything go through if he isn't satisfied with it himself.

Fred never seems to get frazzled by the amount of work he juggles every day. Though other child actors might not be able to juggle working on a weekly show, filming movies, keeping up with schoolwork, *and* appearing regularly on TV award and talk shows, Fred seems to handle everything just fine.

He is very mature for his young age and knows what he likes. The truth is, he is enjoying his stardom.

He's levelheaded and responsible. He gives his family complete credit for helping to make his acting dream come true.

Fred enjoys a quiet life-style when he is away from the spotlight. He says his best quality is his total honesty. He cares about people's feelings and emotions, and friendship is very important to him. It's something he treasures, and he tries to stay in touch with all his friends.

What is Fred's definition of a true friend? "The thing I look for most in a person is if they are thoughtful and respectful," he says. "If someone makes fun of you, a good friend will be on your side and stick up for you. I guess loyalty is also important."

During the last year the Savage family bought a house in the San Fernando Valley while keeping their home in Glencoe, Illinois. With the acting bug spreading throughout the Savage household, it was necessary to move to the sunny state. All three Savage kids are acting on California-based shows.

The new house has a swimming pool, and Fred has his own room. It's the main reason, he says, why he has gotten so used to his new surroundings so fast. "I love it," he says. "Chicago will always be my home, because I grew up there. But L.A. is great."

Inside Fred's bedroom he has a teddy bear and stuffed Roger Rabbit sitting on his bed. Over his desk he has a bulletin board, which he has filled with photos and buttons of his favorite baseball players. On his desk he keeps his current schoolwork and the latest *Wonder Years* script.

Next to Fred's bed there is his favorite possession—his telephone. And on the other side of the room is Fred's stereo and CD player. He says it's great to go into his room, close the door, and just relax. He can play his stereo if he wants to and not bother his brother, whom he used to share a room with.

The only problem is, Fred misses his dad, who hasn't left his job in Chicago. On weekends Lew Savage flies to California to spend two days with his family. During hiatus Fred and his family all move back to their home in Glencoe. For only two months out of the year, the Savage family live together in the same house. Although Fred loves the work he is doing, being separated from his dad is the hardest thing to adjust to.

Another thing he's been having trouble getting used to are the braces he recently got. They are partially removable, but Fred still says, "Every time I have them on, they cause me to slur my *s*'s."

In just a short time, Fred has become a well-known celebrity—so well-known that he was invited by First Lady Barbara Bush to a ball during the inaugural. "I couldn't go because I was working," he says, "but I have the letter on White House stationery framed in my room."

Fred was also asked to serve as grand marshal for the Mardi Gras festival in New Orleans, Louisiana, and had a great time. About that experience Fred exclaims, "I've never seen anything like it before!"

Even though he maintains a very busy schedule, Fred still manages to donate time to charities. He takes part in the Famous Phone Friends organization, for which he makes surprise phone calls to cheer up chronically ill kids.

He also speaks out to kids about drugs. Like many other teen stars, Fred feels very strongly about encouraging kids to stay away from drugs. He even appeared in Chicago's "Just Say No to Drugs" parade last year.

Probably the most surprising thing about Fred is that he likes to baby-sit neighborhood children twice a week to earn some extra money. "I'm supposed to get a weekly allowance of about nine dollars, but one of my worst habits is biting my nails," offers Fred. "So the deal is, if my nails are long, I'll get an allowance. I never have to beg my parents for money because I have the money I earn from baby-sitting."

As Fred's popularity keeps growing, his brother and sister have had to deal with star-struck kids in school. "People ask me in school if I'm Fred's brother," says Ben. "And when I say I am, boys ask me if he is nice, and girls ask me where I live."

Yet, while many girls dream of Fred as their one and only teen favorite, his sister Kala has color pinups of Wil Wheaton in her bedroom. "She's a big fan of Wil Wheaton," expresses Fred. "She *loves* him."

Lately Fred has experienced more and more fans

coming up to him in public asking for his autograph. "I don't know how they do it," he says. "I always think of myself in their situation. If I saw someone famous, I could never go up to them and say, 'Can I have your autograph?' What if they said, 'No'?"

Because Fred would hate being rejected by one of his favorite stars, he would never disappoint a fan who wants his autograph. Fred is consistently gracious when someone stops him and asks him a question. One night Fred and his family got all dressed up and went out to eat. The waitress took one look at Fred and told him she knew him from somewhere. When he proceeded to list everything he had ever done, she said, "I know. You were great in *Flight of the Navigator*." Fred answered politely, "That was someone else," to which the waitress replied, "You were good in it anyway."

Does Fred like being the center of attention? He says he doesn't mind it. Does he feel as if he missed out on a regular childhood? Again, he is honest. "Sure I missed out on a few things," he remarks. "But when people come up to me and tell me how *The Wonder Years* is the story of their lives and that the show helps them remember the good times, it makes me happy I'm doing something good. Besides, I know that out there in this world are kids just like me who would be glad to give up the few things I'm missing to get to do the things I'm doing."

Fred thinks there are more advantages to being in

show business than disadvantages. "I get to meet famous people, go to fantastic places, and do great things that someone my age probably wouldn't get to do," he says.

With all her children working, mom Joanne finds very little time to devote to the things she used to do. For one thing, she is unable to prepare home-cooked meals for her family. There just aren't enough hours in the day to do all the things Fred and his family try to accomplish.

The Savage clan has been eating out a lot and catering food in. Fred says, "I like to try all different kinds of foods, but I still like Italian the best. I love lasagna and pizza. I also love McDonald's—Big Macs, Quarter Pounders, it's great fast food!"

When Fred isn't glued to his TV set watching his favorite show, *21 Jump Street,* he heads to the movies. He loves adventure flicks but also goes to see all dramas and comedies, especially those movies starring Jack Nicholson, Clint Eastwood, and Bette Midler.

For fun Fred likes getting outside on a sunny day. He is an outdoors type who enjoys getting close to nature. Fred could spend hours playing sports or just relaxing in the hot summer sun.

One of Fred's biggest interests and pastimes is music. When he isn't listening to his favorite tunes on the stereo, he's playing his synthesizer and piano. Fred began taking piano lessons at age eight, and he's become a very good player. He has a good ear for music and can pick up the notes of a song just by listening to it on the radio and then play it without the benefit of sheet music.

Traveling is very much at the top of Fred's favorite-things-to-do list. This adventurous young star has seen many different states and countries and wants to see even more. He really enjoys visiting all parts of the world. Of all the places Fred has traveled to, he thinks the Bahamas is the best place to go on vacation.

Fred, who is called Freddy by his close friends and family, has often been asked about his raspy voice. "I have nodules on my vocal cords," he says. "There's nothing wrong. I just can't yell too loud at football games."

Fred tries to go see as many football and baseball games as he can, especially if his favorite teams are playing. He loves the football team the Chicago Bears, and the baseball team the Chicago Cubs.

"I'm a loyal Cubs fan," he says. "I have all their baseball cards. Every time a new player is traded, I add the new cards to my collection."

Superstardom is one of those things everybody wants. Fred has achieved it, but he sees two sides of it. There are pleasures mixed with problems, though in the end it's a very interesting road to be on.

He compares the way he handles his busy life to the comic-book hero Superman. "When I'm back in Chicago, I'm the mild-mannered schoolboy who is not treated any differently from other students. That's my

Clark Kent phase," he grins. "But when I'm in California, that's when I turn into Superman because I'm always on the go, making movies, going to school, and working on the show. I call myself the two faces of Fred."

·12·

ONWARD AND UPWARD

In January 1990 the Pepsi-Cola Company announced a new series of Pepsi television commercials. They decided TV's top teen stars, Fred Savage and Kirk Cameron, should be the company's newest spokesmen.

Fred was chosen because the company recognized him as one of the hottest young stars on TV. He was Pepsi's number-one choice; they believe Fred is perfect to be featured in a string of appealing spots for their product.

Ironically, Fred had left the world of commercials early in his career to pursue acting jobs in movies and television—but now he was being offered a commercial. He liked the idea from the beginning and decided to do the ads for Pepsi. His first commercial is called "Love Letters" and shows Fred getting inspiration from an ice-cold Pepsi to write a love letter to his girlfriend.

The Pepsi commercial was just one of many things offered to Fred in the latter part of 1989. He has become such a popular young actor, he is now on the minds of many producers and casting people. Over the past year Fred not only appeared in various projects, he was also awarded many trophies for his tremendous acting talents.

The Hollywood Women's Press Club honored Fred with the Golden Apple Award for the best male discovery of the year. And he was very pleased to be told he had won the People's Choice Award for favorite young TV performer.

Fred, who hosted the show with Valerie Harper and Barbara Mandrell, got an unexpected surprise when Bob Saget (*Full House, America's Funniest Home Videos*) brought on a video of Fred on Christmas morning at age five. The cute second of tape was courtesy of Fred's mom and dad, whom he thanked in his acceptance speech. He also thanked his agent, Iris Burton, his brother and sister, and all the people who voted for him.

A personal accomplishment for Fred this past year was making his bar mitzvah over the Thanksgiving weekend. A bar mitzvah is a ceremony in the Jewish religion for a boy turning thirteen years old. It is customary for the boy to read sections of the book Torah and deliver an address inside a synagogue. The ceremony symbolizes the boy's entry into manhood.

Last season, in one special episode of *The Wonder Years,* Kevin's friend Paul celebrated his bar mitzvah. In real life the actors who portray the roles, Fred and Josh Saviano, had their own bar mitzvahs during the same year. Josh's ceremony was first, taking place on his birthday in his home in New York.

Although Fred's thirteenth birthday was on July 9, the Savage family decided Fred's celebration would be over the Thanksgiving weekend when Fred had some time off. The four-day party was planned months in advance.

First, the engraved invitations were mailed out to all Fred's *Wonder Years* costars, and relatives and friends from his home in Glencoe. The invitations, sent by Mr. and Mrs. Savage, read, "Please share our joy at the bar mitzvah of our son Fred."

When everyone had arrived on Thanksgiving Day, the festivities began. A buffet dinner, including the traditional turkey and stuffing, was served to guests at the Savage home in California. The next morning at ten A.M. everyone met at Universal Studios for a special guided tour of the famous Universal lot. On Saturday the special guests joined the Savages at the Stephen S. Wise Temple in Los Angeles at five-thirty P.M. for the religious ceremonies. Finally, on Sunday the party continued until after brunch was served. It had been a memorable weekend for Fred.

The feeling of beginning his teenage years made Fred wonder about what the future holds for him. Today the young star is at a very crucial time in his life. His outlook on his career is a simple one—he enjoys acting and looks forward to doing future projects. He wants to be given the chance to expand and broaden his horizons. According to Fred, it is important to play a variety of different roles to demonstrate his versatility as an actor.

Fred feels fortunate that he has been given the opportunity to play various roles in movies. So far he hasn't repeated himself, and he doesn't intend to. He is anxious to do another motion picture, provided it is something completely different from his last role in *The Wizard*.

Fred thinks he has found the right part, and if all goes well, it looks certain that he will bring the comic-book character Richie Rich to life in a live-action movie. It will be filmed during his hiatus from *The Wonder Years*.

This show has a very special place in Fred's heart, and he doesn't see himself leaving the series anytime in the near future. He would rather continue working as he has done for the past two years, filming movie projects during his month off. Fred realizes that *The Wonder Years* was his initial big break in the business. He thought he had achieved recognition for his work before the show came his way, but now he knows it was *The Wonder Years* that brought him to the forefront. It's allowed him to polish his acting abilities by giving him a nice range of situations to work with.

Fred has accomplished just about everything he's always dreamed about. His career is well established, and his personal life is happy and content. Fred could stop working now and always be remembered as the boy who did it all. But he plans on going further.

Stardom has given Fred the one thing every actor hopes for—the chance to always be working. He has a burning desire to keep acting. Fred isn't the type who does anything halfway. Once he is committed to a project, he gives it his all. He feels you have to be serious about what you are doing; otherwise, no one will take you or your work seriously.

Acting is very self-fulfilling for Fred. When he thinks ahead to his future, he says, "I'm still young to decide what I want to be for the rest of my life, but so far I want to be an actor."

Whatever he decides to do in the years ahead, one thing is certain: Fred Savage loves taking chances, and with this kind of determination, he will definitely achieve every goal he sets for himself.

FRED'S VITAL STATS

FULL REAL NAME: Fred Aaron Savage

BIRTHDATE: July 9, 1976

BIRTHPLACE: Highland Park, Illinois

HEIGHT: 5'

WEIGHT: 90 lbs.

HAIR COLOR: Brown

EYE COLOR: Brown

FAMILY: Parents, Lew and Joanne; younger sister, Kala; younger brother, Ben

FIRST AMBITION: To be a professional baseball player

FAVORITE ACTORS: Jack Nicholson, Clint Eastwood

FAVORITE ACTRESS: Bette Midler

FAVORITE MOVIES: All adventure movies, especially *Raiders of the Lost Ark*

FAVORITE TV SHOW: *21 Jump Street*

FAVORITE SINGERS: Paula Abdul, Whitney Houston, Prince, Michael Jackson, Def Leppard

FAVORITE COLORS: Pastels

FAVORITE SPORTS: Baseball, football, and tennis

FAVORITE BOOKS: *A Tree Grows in Brooklyn, Treasure Island, Tom Sawyer*

FAVORITE VACATION SPOT: The Bahamas

FAVORITE FOODS: Italian, McDonald's

FAVORITE CAR: Ferrari, Porsche

FAVORITE SCHOOL SUBJECT: Science

MUSICAL INSTRUMENTS PLAYED: Piano, clarinet

HOBBIES: Collecting baseball cards and World War II pins

MOST PRIZED POSSESSIONS: "An autographed baseball of the Brooklyn Dodgers and my grandfather's war pins and awards."

IDEAL GIRL: "Someone nice, friendly, and easy to talk to. Someone with a good sense of humor."

IDEAL DATE: "Going to the movies and to dinner. Just having fun!"

SELF-DESCRIPTION: "Funny, energetic, friendly, nice, and fun to be with.

WORST HABIT: "Biting my nails!"

BIGGEST LIKES: Music and sports

BIGGEST DISLIKE: Getting a C in school

LITTLE-KNOWN FACT: Fred has never studied acting.

BIGGEST INFLUENCE ON HIS LIFE: "My mom. She's been so supportive of my career," he says.

WHERE TO WRITE TO FRED: Fred Savage
% *The Wonder Years*
ABC-TV
2040 Avenue of the Stars
Los Angeles, CA 90069

FRED SPEAKS OUT

ON HIS ROLE, BRIAN STEVENSON, IN *LITTLE MONSTERS*

"**B**rian is a regular kid like me. The only difference is he's just moved to a new city and he's going through troubles. He's kind of disoriented, and he's trying to make new friends. Actually, Brian isn't afraid of monsters, and I always leave the night-light on."

ON OTHER ACTORS

"**Y**ou see them all day, every day, and you're with them all the time, and they become friends with you. Everyone has been nice so far."

ON HIS SENSE OF HUMOR

"**I**'m a good audience for jokes, even the dumbest ones. I'm easily amused. I also like to crack some jokes of my own."

ON HIS IDEA OF A PERFECT DAY

"**M**y perfect day would be at a baseball-card shop with a charge account!"

ON HIS FRIENDS

"They feel good for me. They don't treat me any better or worse. I have known most of my friends since I was two years old. They knew me before I started acting, and they just treat me like they always did. Some people look at me and think I'm this big star. But to my friends at home, I'm just plain ol' Fred."

ON FANS

"I'm not so swamped that I can't go out of the house, but people do recognize me on the street. They usually stop and ask me, 'Aren't you that boy from *The Wonder Years*?' They want your autograph. It's nice to get support from people who watch the show."

ON HIS FAN MAIL

"Some of the letters say, 'We really like your show, and you're really good.' But then others say, 'Oh Fred, you're so cute. I love you so much.' "

ON HIS CHILDHOOD MEMORIES

"My best childhood memory was when I got my first bike and learned to ride it. My worst was when I broke my leg at four years old. We just got this new bouncy tube, and I was showing my mom all the ways I could fall off it and not hurt myself. But I landed wrong and broke my leg. I had to wear a cast for two and a half months."

ON HIS MOM AND DAD

"My dad is the dominant one, and Mom is the quiet one. But Mom's the one who will send me to my room."

ON PLAYING AN EMOTIONAL SCENE

"It's really pretty easy to do. You just pretend you're in the same situation, and you say the words with the same feeling that you would if you really were in the situation. It comes naturally after a while."

ON HAVING A GIRLFRIEND

"I used to have a girlfriend a year ago, but now we're just good friends."

ON CHANGES

"Since I started on *The Wonder Years,* we bought a house in California, which I love. It's the first time I have my own bedroom. Up until now I was sharing with my brother. But now I have a room all to myself, and it's so cool to be able to go up, shut the door, and play my stereo. The only other big change I've undergone since the show started is that I'm taller."

ON HIS PERSONALITY

"On a scale from one to ten, one being Beaver and ten being Dennis the Menace, I'd say I'm a five."

ON HIS PET PEEVES

"I don't like getting up early. And I hate ketchup. I have a cousin who puts ketchup on everything—eggs, pancakes, all of that."

ON HIS FUTURE GOAL

"I was already nominated for an Emmy award. My future goal is to win an Emmy or an Oscar."

Fred's Filmography

The Boy Who Could Fly
(1986)

DIRECTED AND WRITTEN BY Nick Castle
PRODUCED BY Gary Adelson
COPRODUCER: Richard Vane
ASSOCIATE PRODUCER: Brian Frankish
PHOTOGRAPHED BY Steven Poster
RELEASED BY Twentieth Century-Fox
STARRING Jay Underwood, Lucy Deakins, Bonnie Bedelia,
     Fred Savage, Fred Gwynne, Colleen Dewhurst, and
     Louise Fletcher.

The Princess Bride
(1987)

DIRECTED BY Rob Reiner
SCREENPLAY BY William Goldman, based on his novel
EXECUTIVE PRODUCER: Norman Lear
PRODUCED BY Andrew Scheinman
ASSOCIATE PRODUCERS: Steve Nicolaides and Jeffrey Stott
MUSIC BY Mark Knopfler
PHOTOGRAPHED BY Adrian Biddle
RELEASED BY Twentieth Century-Fox
STARRING Carl Elwes, Mandy Patinkin, Chris Sarandon,
     Fred Savage, Christopher Guest, Wallace Shawn,
     Robin Wright, Peter Falk, Carol Kane, Peter Cook,
     Billy Crystal, and Andre the Giant.

Vice Versa

(1988)

DIRECTED BY Brian Gilbert
EXECUTIVE PRODUCER: Alan Ladd, Jr.
WRITTEN AND PRODUCED BY Dick Clement and Ian
    Frenais
MUSIC BY David Shire
PHOTOGRAPHED BY King Baggot
RELEASED BY Columbia Pictures
STARRING Judge Reinhold, Fred Savage, Swoosie Kurtz,
    and David Proval.

Little Monsters

(1989)

DIRECTED BY Richard Alan Greenberg
WRITTEN BY Terry Rossio and Ted Elliott
EXECUTIVE PRODUCERS: Mitchell Cannold and Dori B.
    Wasserman
PRODUCED BY Jeffrey Mueller, Andrew Licht, and John A.
    Davis
PHOTOGRAPHED BY Dick Bush, B.S.C.
MUSIC BY David Newman
RELEASED BY MGM/UA
STARRING Fred Savage, Daniel Stern, Margaret Whitton,
    Ben Savage, Kala Savage, Rick Ducommun, and
    Howie Mandel.

The Wizard

(1989)

DIRECTED BY Todd Holland
EXECUTIVE PRODUCER: Lindsley Parsons, Jr.
PRODUCED BY David Chisholm and Ken Topolsky
WRITTEN BY David Chisholm
MUSIC BY J. Peter Robinson
PHOTOGRAPHED BY Robert Yeoman
RELEASED BY Universal
STARRING Fred Savage, Beau Bridges, Christian Slater, Wendy Phillips, Luke Edwards, Jenny Lewis, Sam McMurray, Will Seltzer, and Frank McRae.

TELEVISION APPEARANCES

Fred's first TV commercial was for Pac-Man vitamins at age six. Over the next two and a half years, he filmed over seventy television commercials.

Morningstar/Eveningstar (Fred made his TV debut in this short-lived series. He played Alan.)

The Twilight Zone (guest appearance)

Convicted: A Mother's Story (TV movie)

Run 'Til You Fall (TV movie)

Runaway Ralph (Weekend special)

The Wonder Years (TV series. Fred plays Kevin Arnold)

Saturday Night Live (Fred guest-hosted the late-night show on February 24, 1990)

When You Remember Me (TV movie)

ABOUT THE AUTHOR

GRACE CATALANO is the author of the popular Bantam Starfire books *New Kids on the Block*, *Alyssa Milano: She's the Boss*, and *Richard Grieco: Hot 'n' Cool*. She has written *Teen Star Yearbook* and is currently the editor of three entertainment magazines: *Rock Legend* and the popular teen magazines *Dream Guys* and *Dream Guys Presents*. She also wrote *Elvis—A 10th Anniversary Tribute* and *Elvis and Priscilla*. Grace lives on the North Shore of Long Island, New York.

STARFIRE

Romance Has Never Been So Much Fun!